The CHAIN GANG

"IF YOU'RE THINKING OF TRYING TO ESCAPE — FORGET IT"

Tony Ellis

SPHERE BOOKS LIMITED

First published in Great Britain by
Sphere Books Ltd 1986
27 Wright's Lane, London W8 5SW
Copyright © 1986 by Tony Ellis

TRADE
MARK

Set in

Printed and bound in Finland by WSOY

TO MY DARLING WIFE WHO IS
TURNED ON BY MY LITTLE
DRAWINGS OF WELL-HUNG MEN.

Tony Ellis

"HOW LONG D'YOU SAY YOU'VE BEEN HERE?"

"YES, I SUPPOSE THEY ARE A BIT TOUGHER ON YOU SEX OFFENDERS."

"DAMMIT, MAN! — CAN'T YOU ASK THEM TO PUT SOMETHING IN YOUR COCOA?"

"HE'S SUPPOSED TO TAKE THE MUG-SHOTS BUT HE'S A BIT KINKY."

"YOU'VE MASTERED THE SWING......
NOW CONCENTRATE ON THE DROP."

"I DID IT WITHOUT EUEN TRYING".

"DON'T WORRY UNDULY ABOUT YOUR BALLS....
THEY ALWAYS AIM FOR A DOUBLE-TOP TO START."

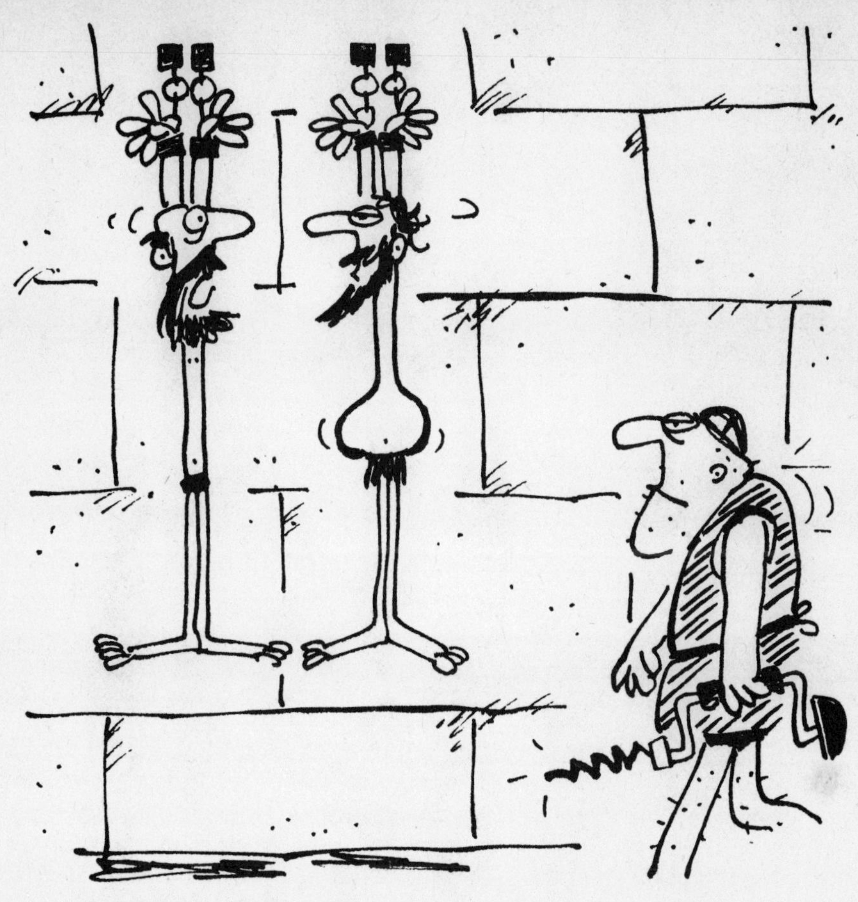

"BLOODY HELL, MAN! YOU DIDN'T TELL THEM YOU WERE CONSTIPATED.....?"

"I'M SORRY YOU DON'T WANT TO JOIN. I'LL ASK YOU AGAIN TOMORROW."

"SOMETIMES I WONDER IF PEOPLE HAVE FORGOTTEN WE EXIST."

"GO ON .... ASK HER ..... SHE CAN ONLY SAY NO!"

"YOU DON'T LIKE ME UERY MUCH DO YOU?"

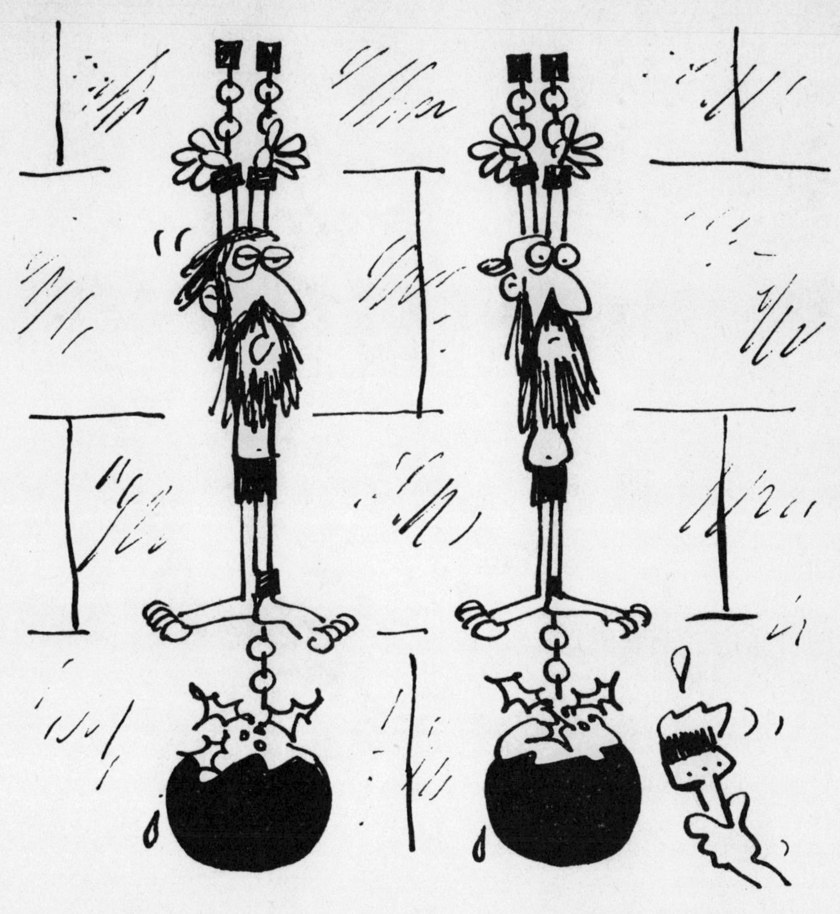

"SHIT, MUST BE CHRISTMAS AGAIN!"

"I SUPPOSE WHAT I MISS MOST IS A
NORMAL SEX LIFE."

"I'M SORT OF LIKE THE BIRD-MAN OF ALCATRAZ — ONLY DIFFERENT."

'YES, IT IS LIKE LOOKING AT TV — ALL REPEATS! WINTER, SPRING, SUMMER, AUTUMN, WINTER, SPRING......."

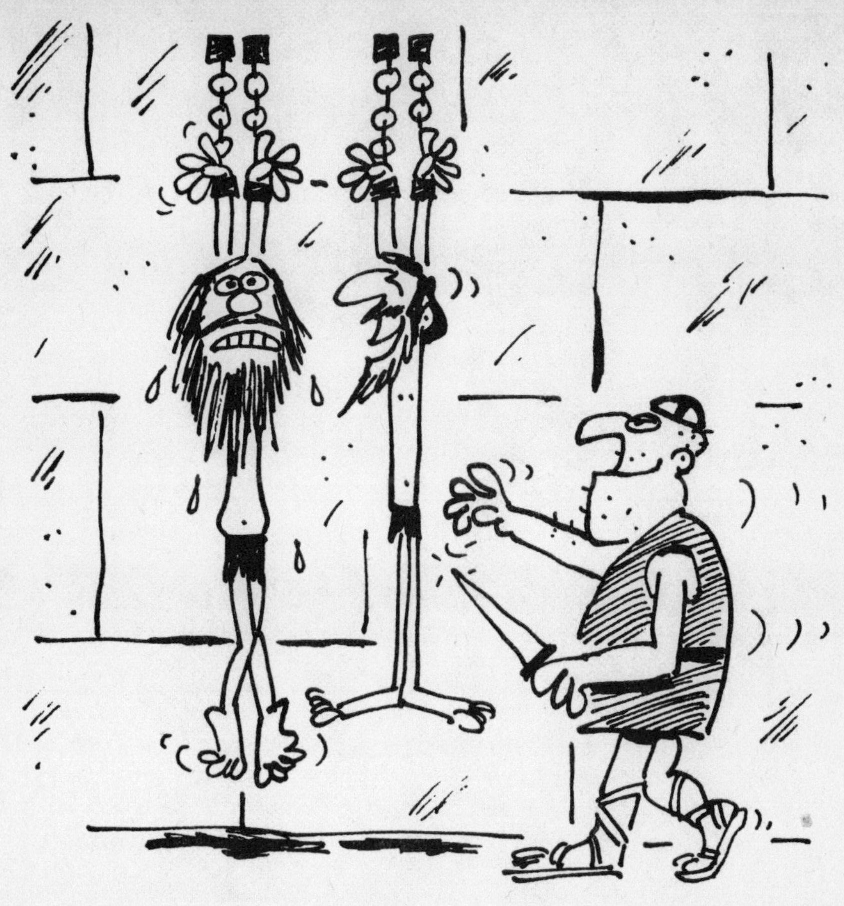

"I PUT YOUR NAME DOWN FOR A SEX-CHANGE OPERATION — I LIKE FEMALE COMPANY".

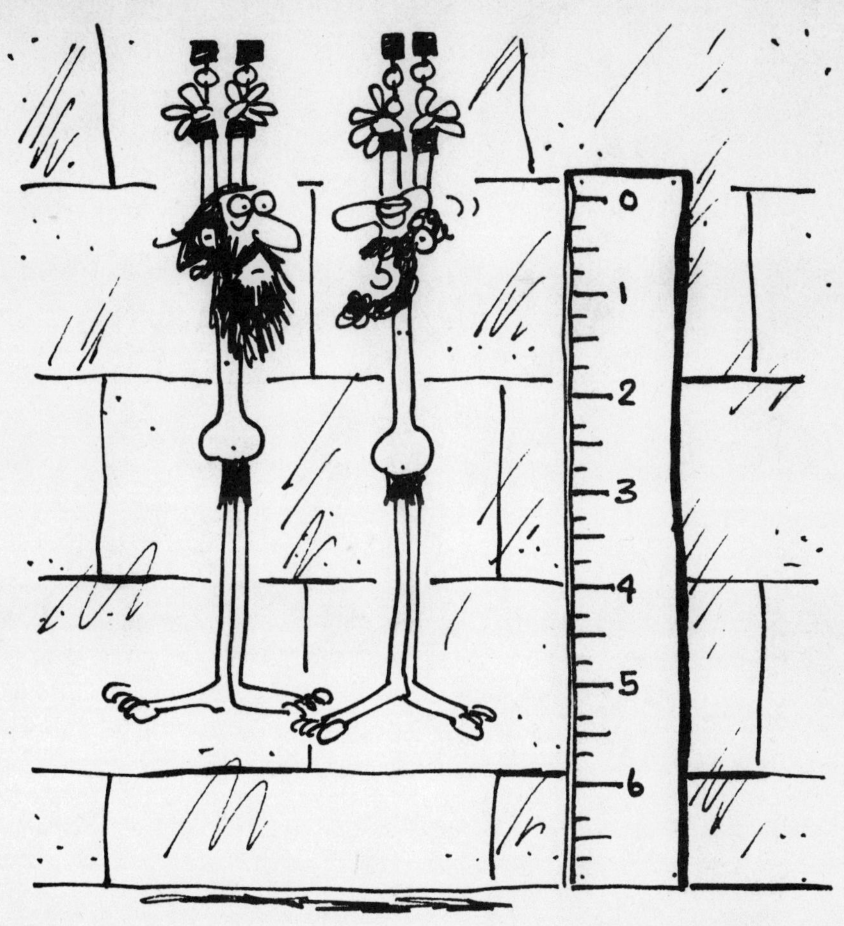

"IT'S A HEIGHT-CHART.....WE GROW DOWNWARDS."

"WE'RE HAVING AN OPEN-AIR HOLIDAY AGAIN THIS YEAR — A FORTNIGHT HANGING OVER THE BATTLEMENTS."

"RELAX. I KNOW IT'S NOT MUCH OF A SEX LIFE, BUT IT'S ALL WE'VE GOT."

"I THINK YOU'RE GOING TO REGRET GOBBING ON THE GUARD".

"WELL, IF THIS IS THE PUNISHMENT BLOCK — IT'S A DODDLE!"

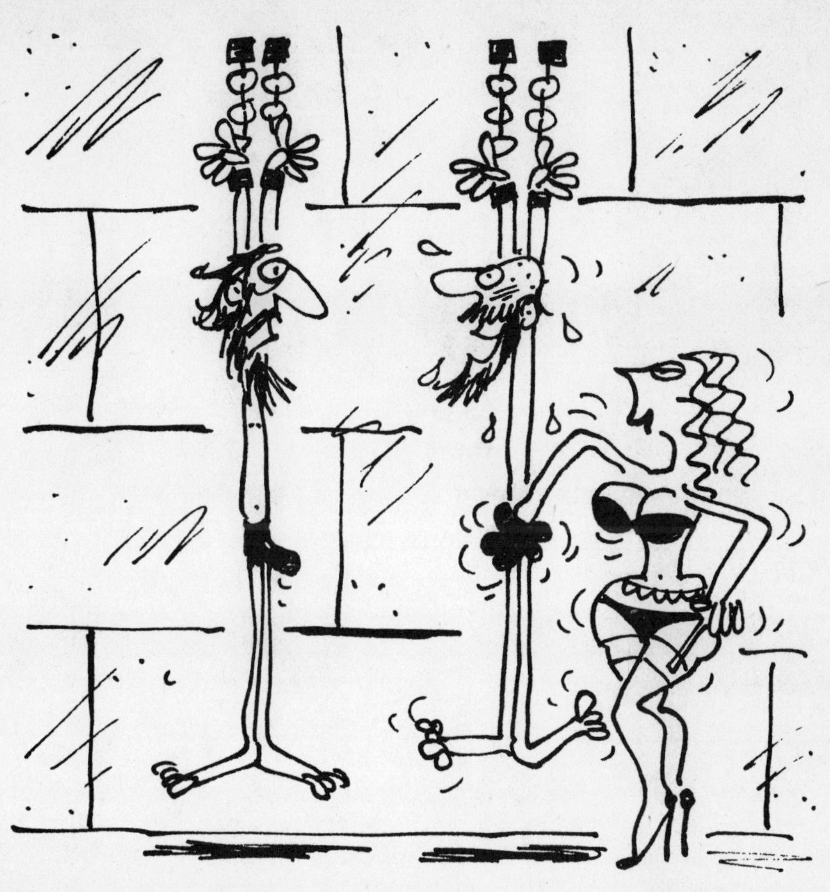

"I DON'T BELIEVE IT, HARRY—AM I DREAMING?"

"IT'S COLD ENOUGH TO FREEZE
THE B......... GOOD LORD!"

"DARNED GOOD SHOES, I'VE HAD 'EM FIFTEEN YEARS WITHOUT A SINGLE REPAIR."

"THEY MUST BE BLOODY JOKING!"

"I SHOULD HAVE BEEN RELEASED IN 1985 BUT THE BASTARDS KEEP PUTTING UP OLD CALENDARS."

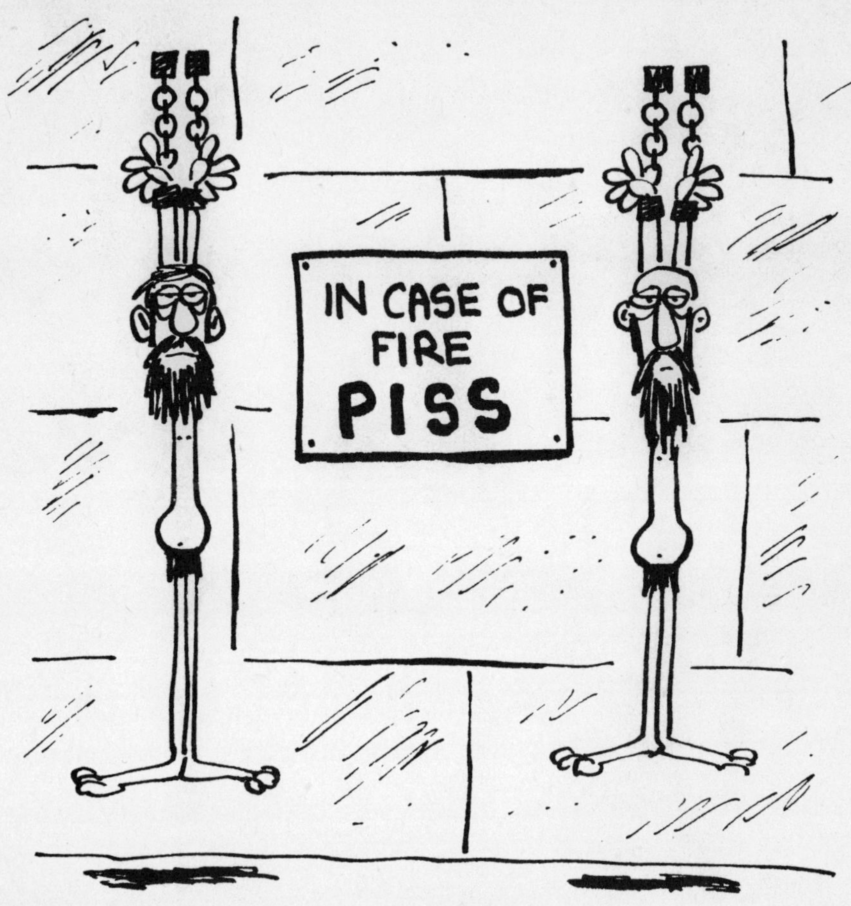

IN CASE OF
FIRE
PISS

"IF PISSING FAILS WE'RE SUPPOSED TO BLEED ON IT."

" IT MUST BE SPRING — THE BATS HAVE
STARTED SCREWING ".

"I HEAR YOU'RE A TOP-SECURITY PRISONER."

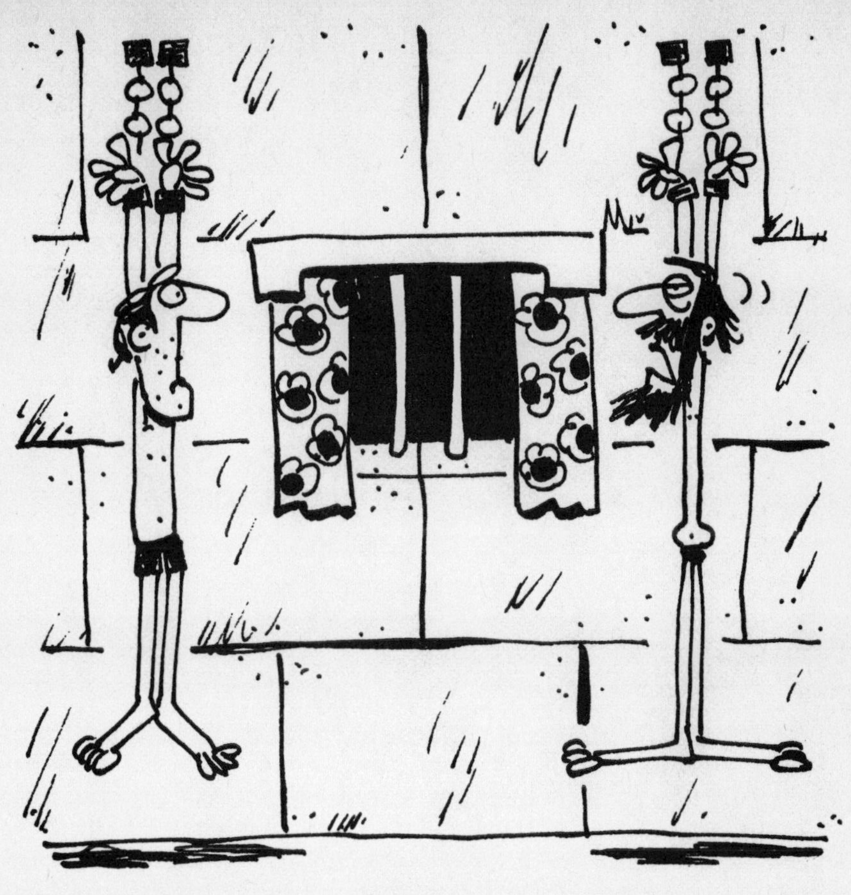

"IT'S THE GOVERNORS WIFE —
SHE'S ROUND THE BEND!"

"IT'S THEIR WAY OF DISCOURAGING SEXY THOUGHTS!"

"A LITTLE DUTCH BOY DID SOMETHING LIKE THIS ONCE ..... BUT HE USED HIS FINGER."

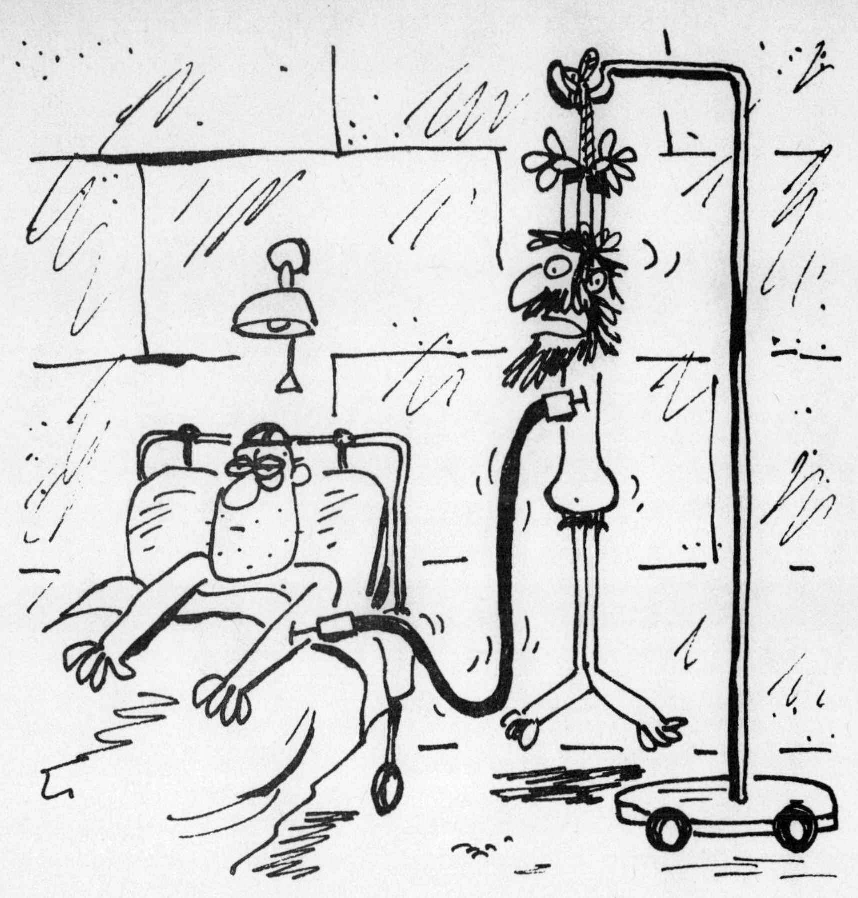

"I DON'T MIND GIVING BLOOD,
BUT THIS IS RIDICULOUS!"

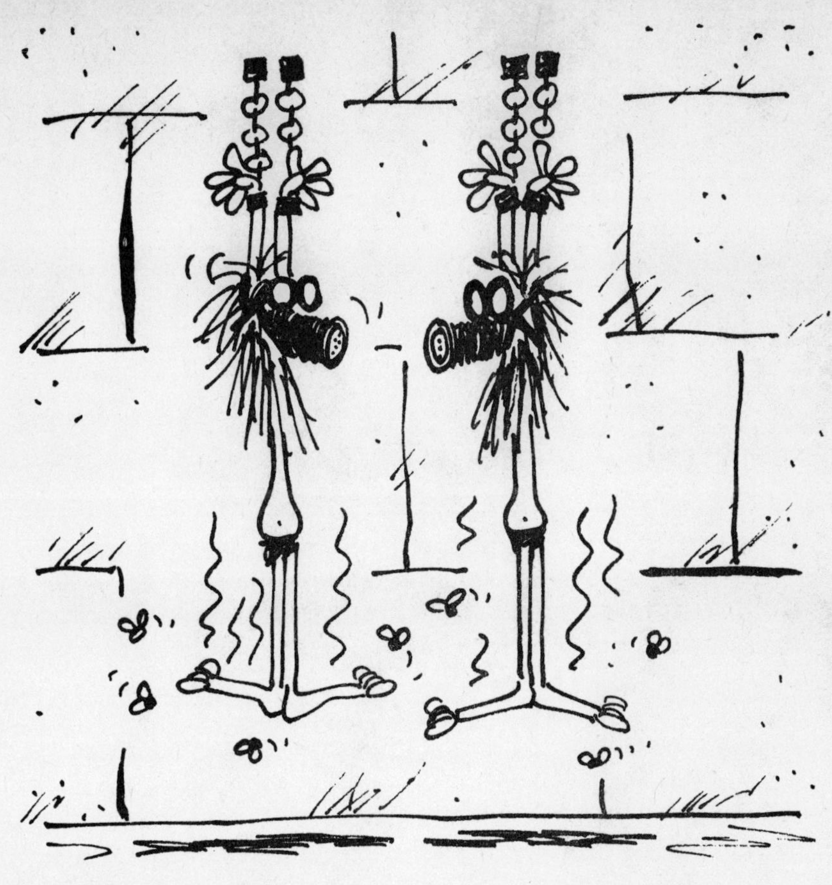

"NICE OF 'EM ...... BUT I WOULD HAVE PREFERRED WASHING FACILITIES."

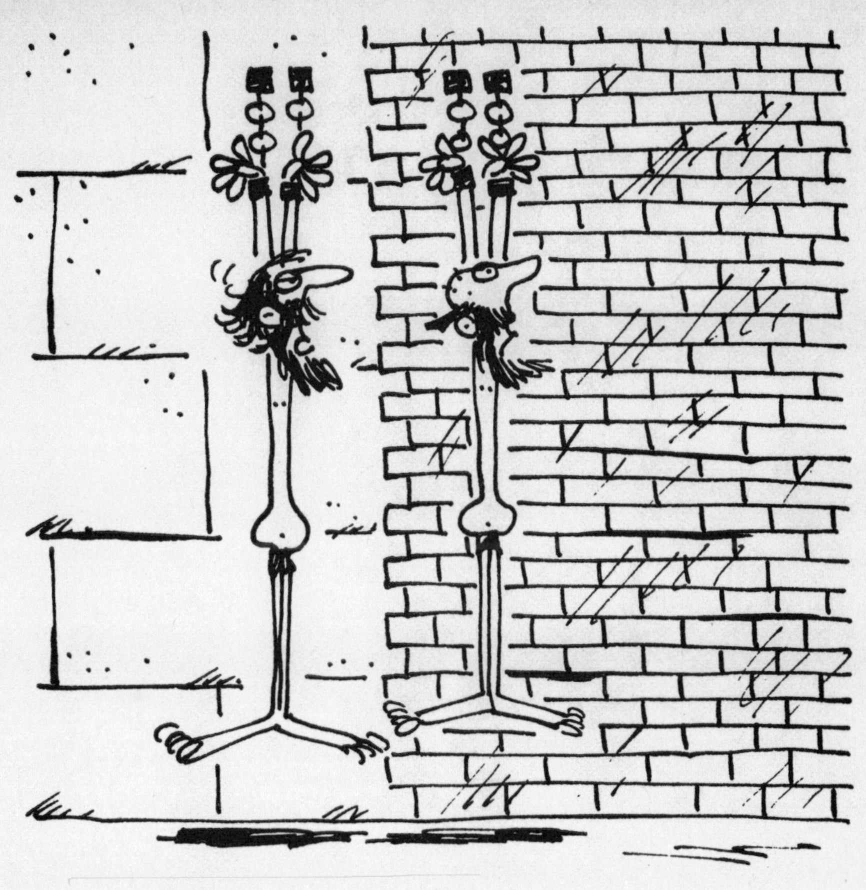

"THE NEW EXTENSION IS OK I SUPPOSE, BUT THE ATMOSPHERE ISN'T THE SAME!"

"SEE THAT? WE'RE FULLY AUTOMATED HERE BURIALWISE."

"I HEAR YOU'RE BRIBING THE GUARD".

"LIFE EXPECTANCY FOR GUYS IN YOUR POSITION IS USUALLY THREE DAYS!"

"THEY CERTAINLY KNOW HOW TO
MAKE A CHAP FEEL MISERABLE."

"IT MUST HAVE BEEN HELL IN THE OLD DAYS!"

"HOLIDAY, MY FOOT! THEY'RE USING
US AS FENDERS."

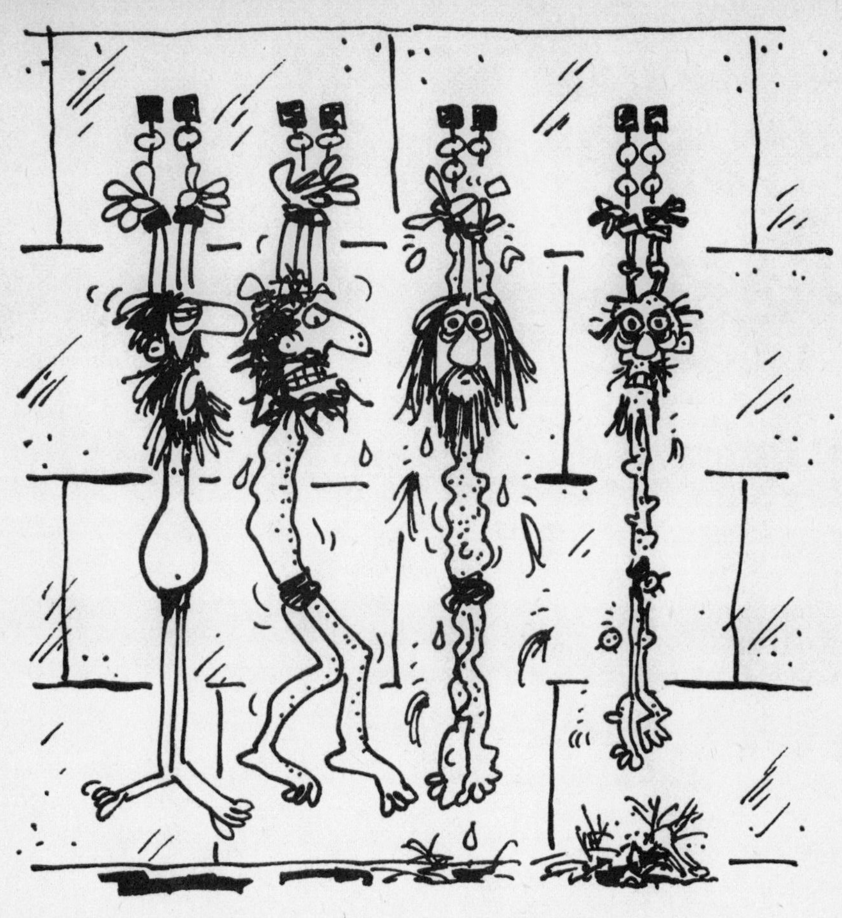

"DAMN! LOOKS LIKE WE'RE IN FOR ANOTHER EPIDEMIC."

"IT IS A NICE GESTURE......IT'D BE EUEN NICER IF THEY PROUIDED A PEN AND PAPER"